VIKING

PRODUCT CREATION

Chapter 1:

Why Product Creation

If you've been looking at starting an online business for a while, you've probably seen several different business models floating around. Probably the most popular one is affiliate marketing. You're told you should use lead magnets and free gifts to build an email list. Stick those lead magnets on a squeeze page and send traffic to it, right? Well, if you've tried it, you've already discovered that it doesn't work very well.

After spending time and/or money on sending traffic to that page, you'll usually notice most people aren't exactly giving you their best email address. In fact, about one-third of them are giving you a fake email. And of the ones that are giving you a real one, it's usually one they reserve for "junk" which is how they think of your promotional material. That means it's an address they don't check regularly and so it's about as useful as a fake one. And keep in mind, they're called freebie seekers for a reason! They don't really buy things. Usually what happens at this point is that a struggling internet marketer starts to realize his or her marketing emails are getting open rates of around 4 or 5% and generating zero sales and that all their effort in creating a lead magnet and landing page and driving traffic was a giant waste. So, they give up on IM and assume it's all a big hoax. Sad story, but it happens every day and it's the ultimate end of about 95% of would-be internet marketers.

So, what are the other five percent doing differently? Easy. They're creating and selling products of their own.

You see, when you create and sell a product of your own, you're creating a different type of list. A buyers list. Unlike freebie seekers who make it a point to never buy anything and also rarely give you their real contact info, buyers actually buy things (crazy right?). These are people who are serious about internet marketing and actually regularly pull out their credit cards and buy things. And because the email you collect comes from their transaction info, you're finally getting real email addresses that people actually check!

And beyond list building, selling your own products carries another benefit. You control your profit. You don't have to split sales revenue with anyone (although you certainly can if you're having affiliates help with a product launch). So, you're either keeping all the profit for yourself or you're choosing how much to share with affiliates. Either way, you're in control.

Furthermore, if you do choose to pay commissions to affiliates and have them drive sales, it's essentially free traffic. You're paying a pre-determined commission to people ONLY when they make a sale, so there's none of the risk or gambling that usually accompanies something like paid display ads or solo ads. You finally switched places with the successful marketers you've been looking up at and now you're letting THEM handle the problem of how to get traffic to YOUR offer. What a difference that makes!

Finally, creating and selling a product establishes credibility like nothing else. In a market packed full of so-called gurus and celebrity marketers, you'll absolutely need credibility. Your credibility affects several things. Firstly, it affects the likelihood of people buying your future products. Secondly, it affects how many people will recognize your name and bother to open your emails. Finally, it boosts your ability to network and recruit affiliates and JV partners. And having a product of your own to point to is one of the quickest and easiest routes to increasing credibility.

You might be asking yourself if product creation is for you. Well, take a moment and look through your inbox right now. Look at all the emails coming in from top internet marketers. Sure, they're all promoting other people's products with affiliate links. But what's the one other thing you see each of them doing at least once every month or two? They're creating and selling their own products. It's very rare that you encounter a successful marketer without their own products. So, if that's the one thing that all successful marketers are doing in your inbox, then guess what: yup, you need to be doing it too. But don't worry. It's easier than you think and there are a ton of different types of products you can make. We'll cover that next.

Chapter 2:
Types of Products

There are a ton of different types of products you can create. In this guide we'll be focusing on digital products because those are the quickest, easiest, and least expensive to make. Digital products are great because you don't have to worry about things like inventory, production costs, wholesalers, warehouses, and shipping. Here's just some of the potential digital products you could create starting right now.

eBooks

Ebooks are an excellent starting place for product creation. They aren't as attractive or likely to convert as video ads or software these days, but they can still be a solid core product and will also come in handy down the road when you're looking to compile bonuses to sweeten the pot on your other product launches. Ebooks can be anything from a how-to guide on a specific tactic or activity to a more general book covering a broad topic in a more general manner. Although ebooks aren't as attractive these days by themselves, they act great as a sub-component of a larger package offer or a companion to a core product like a video course or software.

Video Courses

Video courses have become the new ebook. As of a few years ago, ebooks became old news and people had "banner blindness" when viewing them. The replacement was video courses. Video courses carry a lot of advantages over ebooks. Firstly, people are a lot more likely to consume them. Hardly anyone actually reads the ebooks they purchase these days. They just don't have the time anymore and people these days don't really like reading anyway (thanks public schools!). Video courses can be short and sweet or robust and lengthy. They can be in slideshow format, screen-capture format, or even "talking head" format with you in front of the camera. Generally speaking, a video "course" would be split into a collection of video "lessons".

Reports

Reports don't really hold much weight as paid products these days. They've become the typical free lead magnet. That said, reports can still make good paid products when being used as super low-priced tripwire offers. Also, depending on how snazzy, value-packed, and especially how recent your report is, you might expect it to perform relatively well as a paid product (e.g. if you're publishing Critical Marketing Tends for 2019 right at the end of 2018). Finally, reports do make excellent "added-value" products accompanying more attractive core products like video courses.

PLR

Private Label Rights (PLR) products are another lucrative product category to get into. Essentially, you'd be creating any type of product in any category. But instead of selling it to consumers or "end-users", you'd be selling it to "resellers". They would be receiving a license from you to private label these products. This means they can pretty much pretend they are the authors or creators of these products, rebrand them, edit them, and redistribute them to their own audiences. Because of the nature of PLR and the potential revenue that resellers can expect (not to mention the ease of not having to create their own products) it is often possible to charge premium, high-ticket prices for these licenses.

Swipes and DFY Material

One interesting "miscellaneous" category of products is Swipes and DFY Material. This can be more or less anything that makes a person's life easier or allows them to breeze through an otherwise difficult or time consuming process of their business using materials you provide them. One of the most common of these would be email swipes or "DFY emails". These typically are pre-written affiliate marketing emails or even entire email autoresponder sequences where a person can simply ad their own affiliate links and plug these emails into their own autoresponder. Even a list of subject lines that are proven to lead to high open rates could be a swipe/DFY product. Likewise, a list of top affiliate products to promote, in which you've already done the research on which affiliate offers have the highest conversion rates and the lowest refund rates could be an excellent DFY product. You'll often also see DFY sales pages, DFY sites, and DFY blogs and even DFY social media content like Tweets in this category as well.

Case Studies

Case studies can be an incredibly valuable asset and a super attractive offer. A case study is basically a detailed account of something you accomplished. Specifically, it details how you accomplished it. The steps you took, the processes involved, and –most importantly—the results. You could write a case study about something as little as a successful ad campaign or as robust as a product launch. This sort of product can be delivered in a multitude of formats including a report, an ebook, a video or video course, or an audio file.

Graphics

Graphics collections are a less common but very useful category of products. Graphics are one of those things people usually have to painstakingly learn to do themselves or they have to outsource it to a freelancer for a high price. Bundles of graphics are seen as a low-cost alternative to these two options. Graphics can include banner ad templates, website headers, Facebook page headers, webpage backgrounds, sales page elements, icons, buttons, headlines, avatars, eBook cover templates, logo templates and even collections of stock photos. Document templates can also be included here such as pre-formatted attractive pdf report templates or word document templates with graphical borders or headers and so on.

Software

Probably the hottest trending product category right now is software. Anything that "does something" for you at the push of a button is extremely attractive and has a lot of perceived value. Not too long ago there was a craze where WordPress plugins were all the rage. These are still somewhat popular but have been trumped by cloud-based "Software as a Service" or SAAS platforms which are considered the cream of the crop today. Software can be anything. A landing page builder, a video player, a pop-up script, pretty much anything you can think of that is in-demand that people wish they could do without having to know programming can make a great software.

Interviews

Interviews with successful or famous marketers can be an excellent and very useful product. Interview questions can deal with technical topics like "how do you do Facebook ads" or less tangible topics like motivational advice for entrepreneurs. These interviews could be delivered in any format including text, video, or audio. A good interview product might be a thorough, robust interview with one person or a collection of shorter interviews with several people.

So, there you have it. A ton of great ideas for your next product. Now you've just got to create one! And that's what we'll be talking about next.

Chapter 3:
Making It

So, you may be asking yourself "can I really make my own product?" Don't worry. You're not alone. Most successful product vendors probably wondered the same thing at some point in their past. You'll be surprised by (and very satisfied with) what you accomplish when you put your mind to it. Let's start with written products.

Written Products

So, writing is one of the simplest, most straightforward methods of product creation. If you're making an eBook and you're comfortable writing it yourself, spend a few hours brainstorming what you'll be writing. Make a list of every topic and sub-topic you want to cover and be sure to jot down any random thoughts about points you want to emphasize. Once you've done this, you'll need to shape it into an outline. This is where you'll bring some order and organization to your written product and eventually you'll nail down things like chapter divisions and subsections.

Once you've gotten an outline laid out, it's time to start writing. Two of the most common areas for people to encounter writer's block are the introduction and the conclusion. If you notice you're staring at the same blank page or half-written first sentence after a while, just skip the intro and start writing the "meat and potatoes" of your ebook. Usually you've already got a good idea of what you'll say about specific topics and subtopics so it's often easier to start by knocking these out and there's nothing wrong with doing it this way. You'll want to pay close attention to basic grammar and writing quality here. People have seen plenty of hastily written garbage and you want to make sure your writing sticks out as different and worthy of their time and money. When you're finished writing, be sure to either proofread it yourself a few times or have someone else proofread (a fresh pair of eyes is best).

Finally, once you've got your text completed, you'll want to make your eBook look awesome. There's a few ways to do this. Firstly, decide on a good-looking font for your body, chapter headings and subsection headings. Then, consider adding images or photos throughout. Lastly, you'll want to make the pages themselves look unique. You can either add unique frames/borders or header/footer art and background images/patterns inside of your word processor or you can use a more advanced program like Adobe InDesign to create a truly professional look. Alternatively, you could acquire a sleek, pre-designed template from a site like Envato.

Video Products

Video products are a bit of a mixed bag. On the one hand, they can be quicker to make than written products. On the other hand, they're usually a little more complicated and the software and equipment involved can often be intimidating to someone who hasn't done video before. That said, they are still worth it because videos are seen as considerably more valuable and attractive than textual products. There are a few different types of videos you can do with varying degrees of complexity and equipment requirements.

First, there's the slideshow presentation style. This can be accomplished using any slideshow software. A script isn't strictly necessary for these videos but may make the presentation sound smoother. Unlike eBook writing, where an outline is just the beginning, for slideshow videos the outline is pretty much all of the content! Just narrate the presentation and export it to a video file using your slideshow software or you can just use screen recording software to record your presentation. Sound quality does a lot for perceived value so ensure you're using a quality microphone like Blue Yeti or something similar. To add an extra layer of perceived value to these videos, break from the black on white mold and use a unique background of some sort as well as some images. But here's an expert hint: resist the urge to use all sorts of whacky transitions and animations. Newbies tend to get excited by all the animation and transition options in these slideshow programs and end up going crazy with them but it comes off as cheezy, cliche, and amateur. If you want your presentation to look clean and professional, stick to fades and "slide in" type effects.

Next there's the screen capture style video. This is generally an over-the-shoulder type presentation in which you record your screen and teach how to do something specific. In this case there's usually not a need (nor an opportunity) for a script, but you do want to at least have a general outline of what you're presenting and go through the whole act once or twice to practice and avoid awkward pauses or mistakes. There's several screen recording softwares out there from high-ticket options like Camtasia to free ones like Jing. Some affordable middle-ground options are Snagit and Screencast-o-matic.

Finally, there's the talking head style. This is literally you in front of the camera. This is obviously the one people tend to shy away from the most. Sometimes it's because they don't want to be on camera and sometimes it's because they don't want to worry about cameras and equipment. The fact is, when done right, talking head videos can be super effective at generating trust and brand loyalty, but it's not absolutely necessary. If you are doing a talking head, make sure you use a good lapel mic so your sound quality is good. Also ensure lighting is optimal and either memorize your script or use an excellent teleprompter or teleprompter mobile app. Don't bother with special green screen backgrounds or even super bright white screen backgrounds. 99% of people who mess with this green screen stuff end up wasting money and looking cheesy. A white screen is a little better and more foolproof but still unnecessary. Your office, your backyard, or your couch make a perfectly acceptable backdrop for your videos in most cases (keep it bright and clean, obviously). When you're done shooting, use a video editor like Adobe Premiere to edit and sync the audio to the video (again, use a good lapel mic, not the camera mic).

Software

Software is by far the hottest seller online right now. On any given day, if you look at JVZoo's Top Ten List, you're likely to see a majority of the top products are software tools. Software is seen as having far more value than typical infoproducts. It "does" things for you. It's "magical" and "automatic". Chances are, you aren't a programmer and you can't create your own software from scratch, but it's still very possible for you to create a software product. The quickest way is probably to acquire white label rights to an existing software tool and rebrand it as your own. If you'd prefer to have your own unique software, you can outsource it much more easily than you may think.

Outsourcing Product Creation

Almost any product creation can be outsourced. If you're not much of a writer or you don't have time to write a textual product yourself, there are a ton of writers on places like UpWork and Fiverr. If you want someone else to do your video lessons, whether talking-head, screen capture, or slideshow, there's plenty of talent on those two sites as well. Even software can be outsourced. Don't be afraid to approach freelancers with a rough idea of your dream software. Most freelance programmers can quickly tell you whether what you seek is realistic and how quickly it can be made. Once you've got an idea of how possible it is, present the idea to multiple freelancers and shop around for the best offer.

Chapter 4:

Packaging & Selling It

Once your product is ready, you need to "package" it and get it ready for a launch. We have a more in-depth guide on Product Launching that you can grab once you get to that point, but for now we'll go over some of the basics.

Branding

The first thing you'll need to do is create a brand or identity for your product. You've probably already settled on a name for your product, but if you haven't already, now would be a good time to do some brainstorming. When you do decide on a product/brand name, be sure to do some research and ensure it hasn't been taken. A few searches on google.com and the U.S. trademarks office website should suffice. The next step is to create a logo. This can be done yourself if you're comfortable with basic graphics or logo creation software like Creator 7. Otherwise you can easily outsource this to someone on UpWork or Fiverr. Along with your brand name and image, you'll want to develop a unique selling proposition. What problem does your product solve and why is it better than other alternatives? Come up with a solid USP, preferably no longer than a short paragraph. You won't necessarily be writing this out in your logo or on your sales pages verbatim, although some brands do, but your USP will set the tone for most of your sales copy. So, don't skip this step.

Packaging

So, since we're mostly focused on digital products in this guide, there won't be any physical packaging, obviously. But you'll still need to develop some e-cover images. Really, all you need for this is your logo and a simple ecover software. One great option is myecovermaker.com, but if you are already comfortable with photoshop templates or other solutions, feel free to use those. Ecover creation is pretty straightforward. If your product is an eBook, create an ecover of a book or maybe an e-reader/tablet with your logo on it. If it's a video course, create DVD and/or disk images. And if it's a bundle of multiple product types, make sure they're all represented. You get the idea. Regarding style, you'll want to take into account the theme and colors of your logo and desired brand image. There are no "right or wrong" styles, but it's worth looking at recent top selling digital products to see if there are any trends. For example, these days, the popular style for software products tends to be "clean and minimalist". So, for a software box, you might want an all-white box with your logo centered on it and nothing more. When you're done, take all of your e-cover images and bundle them together on a background table top image. This conveys a feeling of tangible value to your customers.

Product Splintering

If you're hoping to send your customers through a funnel in which they buy a front-end product and then successively more valuable products on the back-end (hint: you should be), then you'll need to splinter your products. This is a way of spreading out the components of one or more products into multiple offers throughout a funnel with varying price points. This often involves a bit of content repurposing too. Here's an example. If you've got a large study course that consists of multiple video lessons and an eBook, with a little bit of work you can turn this into a four-step funnel. First, you can take the intro or first chapter of the ebook, tweak it a little, and turn it into a stand-alone report (alternatively you can just draft up a short report from scratch that summarizes what you're teaching in the main course but provides some value in and of itself). This could be used as a free lead magnet at the entry point of your funnel. Then you could offer the eBook itself as a low-priced front-end or tripwire offer. Then take the video course and make that your core offer or upsell. Finally, on the back-end, you can throw on a profit maximizer such as a 1 hour coaching or strategy session where you walk people through what you're teaching 1-on-1 for a high-ticket price.

You've now gone from a single product to a 4-product funnel.
You get the idea.

Sales Pages

Your sales pages are THE bottleneck of your product's
success. It doesn't matter if you know you have the most
amazing, valuable, life-changing product in the world. If your
sales page isn't converting, you won't succeed. There are a
lot of different approaches to sales pages and copy. Short-
form, long-form, text-only, video-only, and so on. The most
common one's you'll see today are hybrid mid- to long-form
video sales letters. This means a sales page in which the
center of attention is a sales video at the top, under a
headline, and then a long or medium length sales letter below
it that basically repeats the message of the video. This type of
page has the advantage of appealing to people who like to
learn via video, people who like to learn by reading thoroughly,
and people who like to just skim down the page and collect
the main ideas. Whatever style you choose, make sure you
keep it clean looking, attractive, and have every element and
aspect of it point towards your main goal: the conversions.
Ideally, a page like this will have lots of images and sub-
headlines to break up the text. Buy buttons, headlines, and
CTAs should be clear and pop-out easily from the background

(so ensure you use contrasting colors). The overall look and feel of your sales page should ideally match the theme and colors of your brand image. Because a sales page is such a vital part of your success, it's something you should really consider outsourcing if you aren't already good at it.

Accepting Payments

There are several options out there for "taking people's money". You can use your own shopping cart or payment solution like Paypal, ThriveCart, or PayKickstart. Or you can rely on a marketplace like JVZoo, ClickBank, or WarriorPlus. These marketplace/payment processing solutions provide an easy way to list your products, create buy buttons, and manage affiliates all at the same time. If you're doing a "hard launch" with a specific launch period and relying on affiliates, you'll want to take into account what community of affiliates you want to tap into and where they prefer to promote products.

Delivery

So, once you've collected a payment, you'll need an automated method to deliver the product to your buyer. Some marketplaces provide product download or delivery within their platform. Alternatively, you can just forward buyers to your own delivery page with download links or the video lessons and so on. But it's best, these days, to take an extra step towards protecting your content and to lock it behind a members' area. There are several options for this. First, there are the more common WordPress-based options like WishlistMember, MemberMouse, and Digital Access Pass. Then, there are non-WordPress solutions like Kajabi or FreshMember. Whichever you choose, you'll need to go through a few steps to integrate it with your payment platform or marketplace so that people can automatically access their purchases after buying. One other important benefit to membership-based delivery is that it can decrease refund rates. If unscrupulous customers have to login to access materials, they're less likely to request their money back than if they can simply download files to their computer right away.

So, there you have it. A blueprint for creating, branding, and delivering any product you want. But guess what? It's all worthless if you don't apply what you've learned. So make sure you implement the following Battle Plan today:

Battle Plan

Step 1: Determine what type of product you'll create.

Step 2: Brainstorm and develop an outline of your product if it's text or video. If it's software, draft up an overview of its desired features.

Step 3: Start creating your product using the steps above or outsource it to freelancers.

Step 4: Establish a name, brand image, and USP (take care to deconflict with similar brands).

Step 5: Package your product in accordance with your brand image using an eCover creator tool.

Step 6: Get your product ready for customers by linking your members area with your payment platform.